Published By: Augusta Publishing House, LLC.
First Edition: August 2018

I0169277

Name:

Date:

DESCRIBE THE BEST DAY OF YOUR LIFE.

Name:

IF YOU WROTE A BOOK, WHAT WOULD IT BE ABOUT?

Date:

Name:

Date:

WRITE A POEM ABOUT BELIEVING IN YOURSELF.

Name:

Date:

I FEEL MOST CONFIDENT WHEN...

DESCRIBE A TIME WHEN YOU WERE GLAD YOU DIDN'T GIVE UP.

Name:

Date:

IF YOU CREATED YOUR OWN PLANET, WHAT WOULD IT BE LIKE?

Name:

Date:

WHAT WOULD YOU CONSIDER A DREAM COME TRUE?

Name:

Date:

WRITE A STORY ABOUT A STUDENT WHO OVERCAME A CHALLENGE.

Name:

Date:

WHAT INSPIRES YOU?

Name:

IF YOU COULD CREATE A MOVIE, WHAT WOULD IT BE ABOUT?

Date:

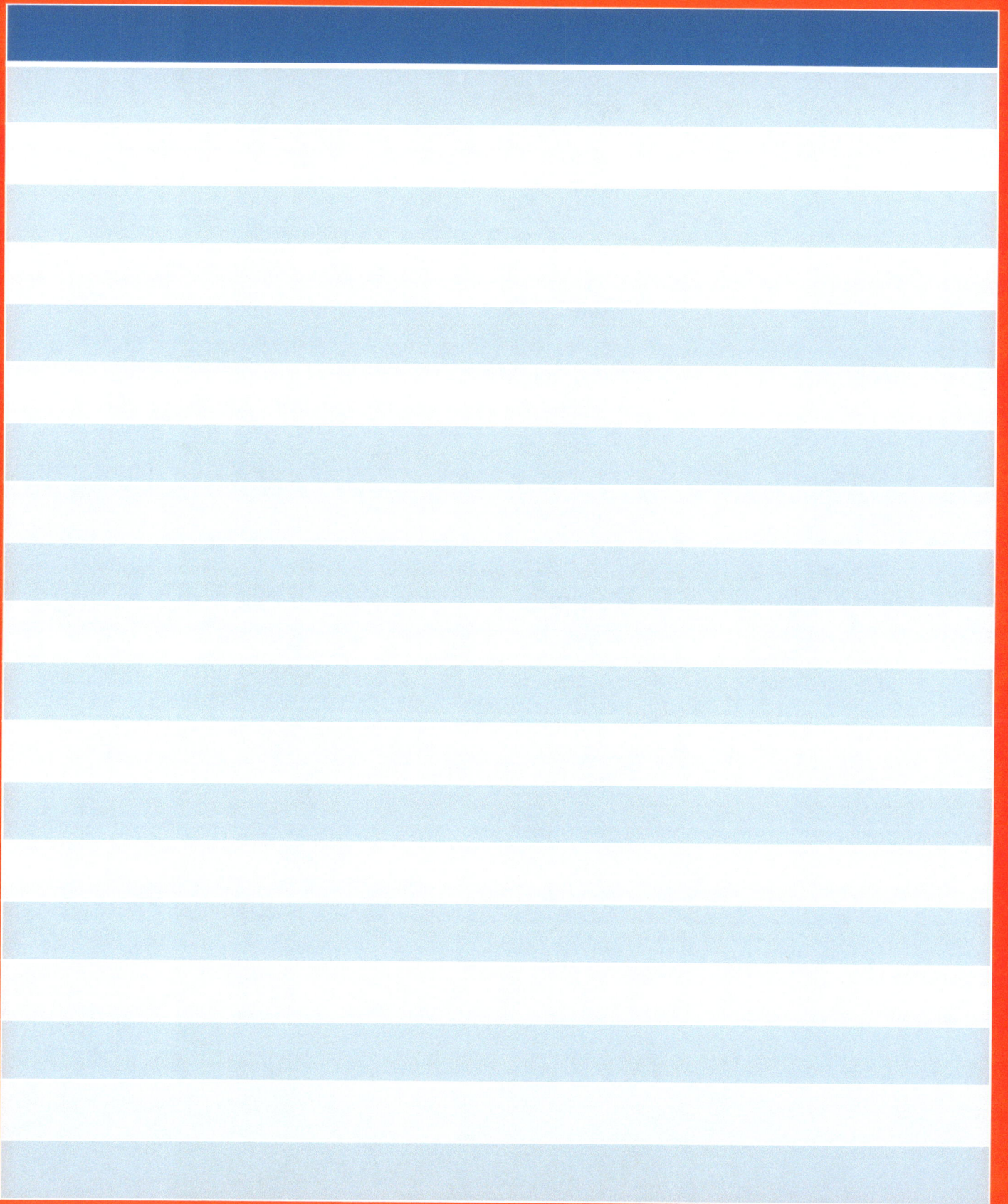

Name:

Date:

WHAT ARE YOU MOST PROUD OF?

IF YOU COULD CHOOSE ONE SUPERPOWER, WHAT WOULD IT BE? WHY?

Name:

WRITE A SHORT STORY ABOUT A KID WHO LEARNED TO BE BRAVE.

Date:

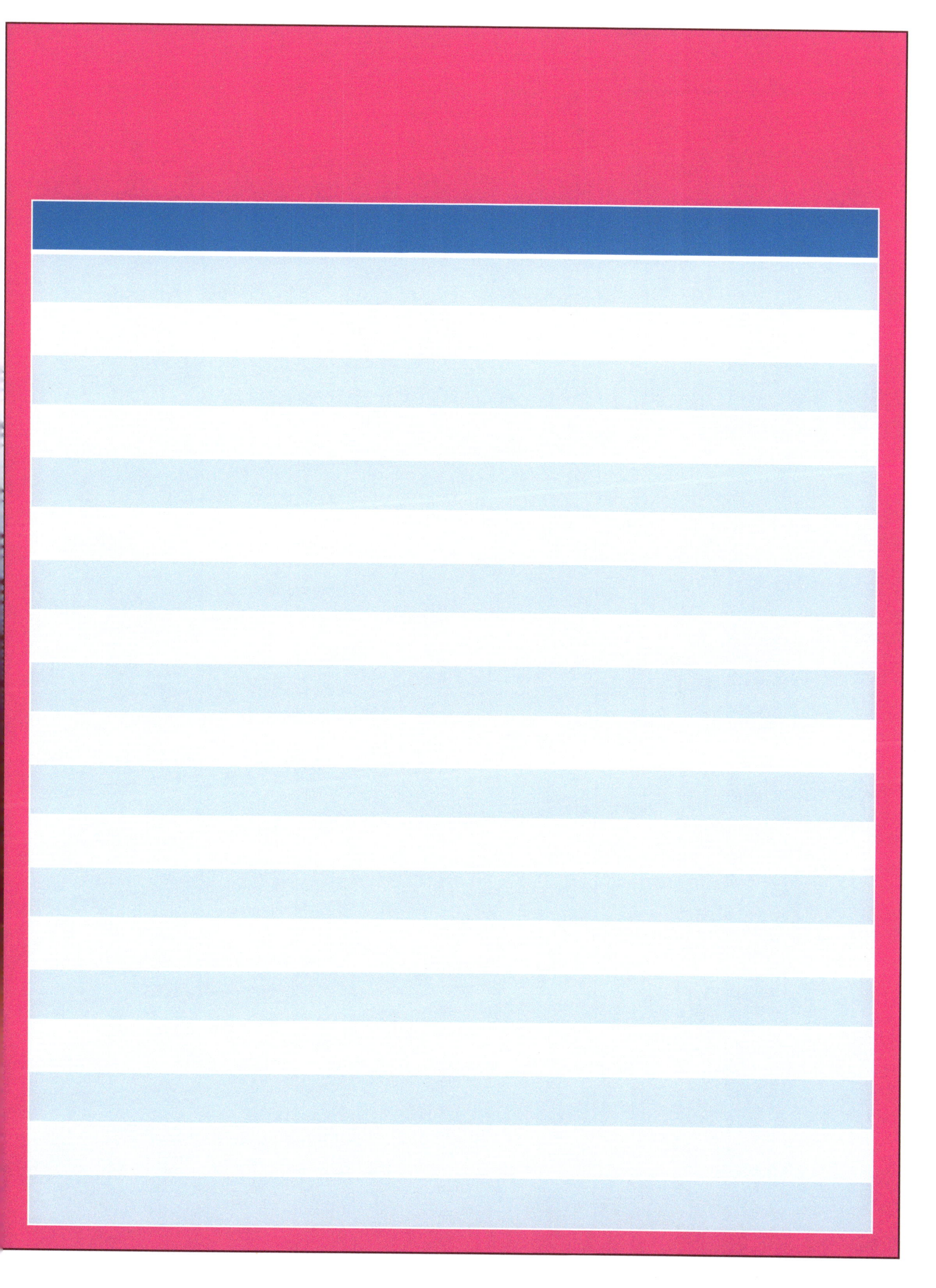

Name:

Date:

WRITE ABOUT YOUR FAVORITE HOBBY.

Name:

Date:

YOU ARE PLANNING A DINNER PARTY, WHAT IS ON THE MENU?

Name:

Date:

WHAT CHEERS YOU UP WHEN YOU ARE SAD?

Name:

Date:

IF YOU DISCOVERED YOU COULD FLY, WHERE WOULD YOU GO?

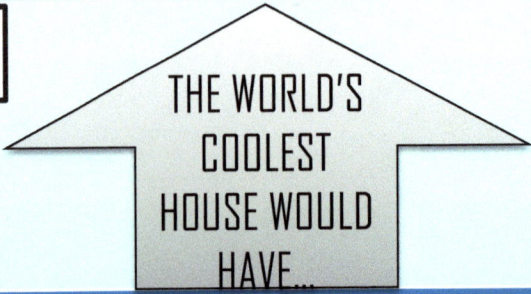

THE WORLD'S COOLEST HOUSE WOULD HAVE...

Name:

Date:

WHAT DO YOU
LOVE MOST ABOUT
YOURSELF?

www.ingramcontent.com/pod-product-compliance
Lightning Source LLC
Chambersburg PA
CBHW040019050426
42452CB00002B/51